W9-COV-659

Gr. 1
Set 6

Bailey's Elementary School

my visit to the
DINOSAURS

HORNED DINOSAU
STYRASCO SAURUS

my visit to the
DINOSAURS

by ALIKI

Thomas Y. Crowell Company   New York

LET'S-READ-AND-FIND-OUT SCIENCE BOOKS

Editors: DR. ROMA GANS, Professor Emeritus of Childhood Education, Teachers College, Columbia University
DR. FRANKLYN M. BRANLEY, Astronomer Emeritus and former Chairman of The American Museum–Hayden Planetarium

LIVING THINGS: PLANTS

Corn Is Maize: The Gift of the Indians
Down Come the Leaves
How a Seed Grows
Mushrooms and Molds
Plants in Winter
Redwoods Are the Tallest Trees
  in the World
Roots Are Food Finders
Seeds by Wind and Water
The Sunlit Sea
A Tree Is a Plant
Water Plants
Where Does Your Garden Grow?

LIVING THINGS: ANIMALS, BIRDS, FISH, INSECTS, ETC.

Animals in Winter
Bats in the Dark
Bees and Beelines
Big Tracks, Little Tracks
Birds at Night
Birds Eat and Eat and Eat
Bird Talk
The Blue Whale
Camels: Ships of the Desert
Cockroaches: Here, There, and
  Everywhere

Corals
Ducks Don't Get Wet
The Eels' Strange Journey
The Emperor Penguins
Fireflies in the Night
Giraffes at Home
Green Grass and White Milk
Green Turtle Mysteries
Hummingbirds in the Garden
Hungry Sharks
It's Nesting Time
Ladybug, Ladybug, Fly Away Home
Little Dinosaurs and Early Birds
The Long-Lost Coelacanth and Other
  Living Fossils
The March of the Lemmings
My Daddy Longlegs
My Visit to the Dinosaurs
Opossum
Sandpipers
Shells Are Skeletons
Shrimps
Spider Silk
Spring Peepers
Starfish
Twist, Wiggle, and Squirm: A Book
  About Earthworms
Watch Honeybees with Me
What I Like About Toads
Why Frogs Are Wet

Wild and Woolly Mammoths

THE HUMAN BODY

A Baby Starts to Grow
Before You Were a Baby
A Drop of Blood
Fat and Skinny
Find Out by Touching
Follow Your Nose
Hear Your Heart
How Many Teeth?
How You Talk
In the Night
Look at Your Eyes*
My Five Senses
My Hands
The Skeleton Inside You
Sleep Is for Everyone
Straight Hair, Curly Hair*
Use Your Brain
What Happens to a Hamburger
Your Skin and Mine*

And other books on AIR, WATER, AND WEATHER; THE EARTH AND ITS COMPOSITION; ASTRONOMY AND SPACE; and MATTER AND ENERGY

*Available in Spanish

Copyright © 1969 by Aliki Brandenberg. All rights reserved. Except for use in a review, the reproduction or utilization of this work in any form or by any electronic, mechanical, or other means, now known or hereafter invented, including xerography, photocopying, and recording, and in any information storage and retrieval system is forbidden without the written permission of the publisher. Manufactured in the United States of America.
L.C. Card 70-78255

ISBN: 0-690-57402-9 (LB)

my visit to the
DINOSAURS

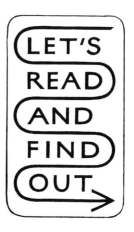

Yesterday I went to see the dinosaurs.
I went with my father and my little sister.
The man showed us where to find the dinosaurs.
He took us up in a big elevator.

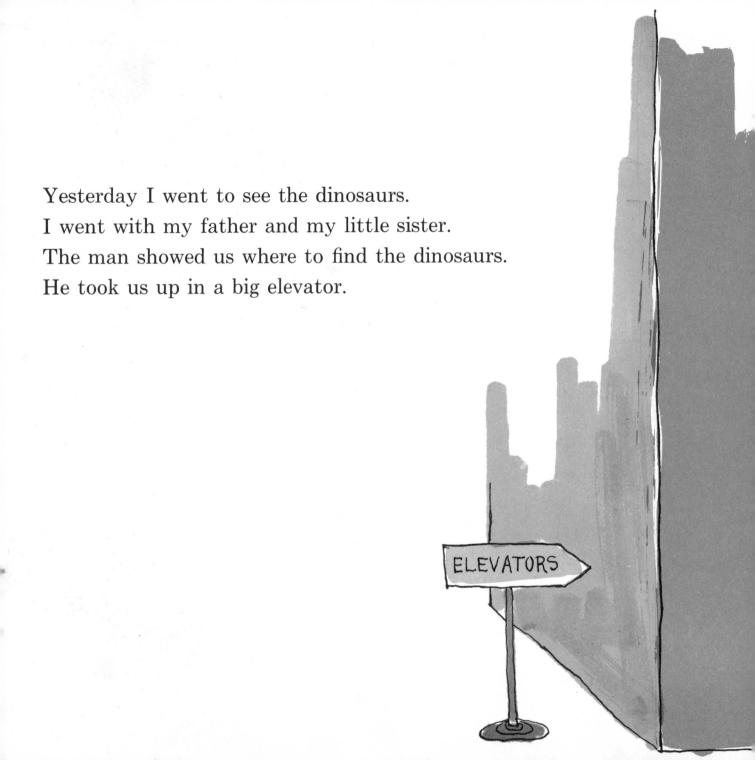

ELEVATORS

VISIT THE
DINOSAURS

UP
DOWN

1

We walked down a hall, turned a corner—and there
   they were. Skeletons.
Real dinosaur skeletons.
They were standing in a room bigger than a house.
One skeleton was almost as long as the room.
It looked scary.

My father told my sister and me not to be afraid.
Dinosaurs lived millions of years ago.
No dinosaurs are alive today.

I took a picture of the long dinosaur,
   BRONTOSAURUS.
Then I went over and looked closer.

The skeleton was wired together. Heavy rods held
   it up.
I could see that some of the bones were not real.
They were made of plaster.
What a job it must have been to put this huge
   puzzle together.
How could anyone know where all the pieces fit?

When the dinosaurs died, they were covered with sand and mud. They were buried for millions of years.

The sand and mud turned into rocks, and the dinosaurs' bones became fossils.

In 1822 the first dinosaur fossil was found.
It was found by accident.

After that, many diggers went looking for fossils.
They dug in the rocky earth.

They found fossil bones of dinosaurs.

Some diggers found fossil eggs, which the dinosaurs had laid in sandy pits.

They even found fossil baby dinosaurs.

It is hard work to take fossils from the ground. They are often embedded in solid rock.

Paleontologists studied the fossils carefully.

A paleontologist is a scientist who studies animals and plants of the past.

Paleontologists know when dinosaurs lived and how dinosaurs lived.

They know what dinosaurs ate.

Some dinosaurs ate meat, and some ate plants.
Giant dinosaurs and duckbill dinosaurs ate plants.
So did horned dinosaurs and armored dinosaurs and plated dinosaurs.
Many of the plant eaters spent most of their lives in the water.

CORYTHOSAURUS
(DUCK BILL DINOSAUR)
PLANT EATER

STYRACOSAURUS
(HORNED DINOSAUR)
PLANT EATER

ANKYLOSAURUS
(ARMORED DINOSAUR)
PLANT EATER

BRONTOSAURUS was a plant eater.

This is the way it looked when it was alive.

Brontosaurus reached down with its long neck in
the swamps and ate water plants.

It could lie low and hide from an enemy.

Its eyes were high on its flat head.

It could peek out without being seen.

BRACHIOSAURUS was another giant dinosaur
that lived in the water and ate plants.
It was the biggest and heaviest dinosaur there ever
was.

Another plant eater was TRACHODON, a duckbill.
It had feet that were webbed, like a duck's.
It was a good swimmer.

Trachodon had jaws shaped like a duck's bill.
The jaws were full of teeth.
Trachodon had 1,600 flat teeth to crush and grind
its food.

17

PROTOCERATOPS was a horned dinosaur.

ANKYLOSAURUS was an armored dinosaur.

These dinosaurs ate plants, too, but they lived on
  land.
They looked so unappetizing that meat-eating dinosaurs left them alone.
Who would want to bite their thick, leathery skin,
  covered with bony spikes and plates?

Meat-eating dinosaurs were fast, fierce hunters.

A hungry meat eater like ALLOSAURUS ate any
animal it could find.

It was not even afraid to attack Brontosaurus, which
was twice its size.

Allosaurus ran on two strong legs.

It caught its prey in its short arms and ripped it
apart with big, pointed claws.

Allosaurus ate its food with long, sharp teeth.

21

My father, my sister, and I went to another hall
and looked at more skeletons.
There were so many to see that we had to hurry.

HORNED DINOSAUR

DIPLODOCUS was the longest dinosaur. Its body was so big, and its head and mouth so small, that it had to eat its plant food almost without stopping, in order to satisfy its hunger.

ORNITHOLESTES was a small, swift dinosaur.
Some of the animals it ate were birds.

OVIRAPTOR was another little dinosaur.
It had no teeth at all.
It ate the eggs of other dinosaurs.

We saw a plated dinosaur, fierce-looking
STEGOSAURUS.

It had big, bony plates covering its back, and a
spiked tail to swing at its enemies.

We saw horned dinosaurs, too.
MONOCLONIUS had only one horn.

STYRACOSAURUS had a horn on its nose and a
frill of spikes around its neck.

And TRICERATOPS had three horns on its head—
one on its nose and one over each eye.
A big, fan-shaped bone protected its neck.
My father said Triceratops could defend itself even
against TYRANNOSAURUS REX.
I wondered who Tyrannosaurus Rex was.